Dreaming Success

(Learning Principles)

To

(Realizing Strengths)

Living Success

(Taking Actions)

Vicky V. Choudhary

Foreword

Your life is your own making. Nobody else except for you and only you are the one responsible for your life. You are the driver who controls the haggle heading or way that you take is and will consistently be your own making. However, how would you order your life to the specific way that you need it to take? In what capacity will you go about in molding your fate? In this book, you can hope to become familiar with all the things that you require to know with the goal for you to take a full control of your life.

This page is left intentionally.

Table of Contents

Chapter 1
Taking Charge of Life

When you do not know what you really are, you cannot take charge of your life. In this first chapter, you will get a glimpse of the basics about it and why it is something that you need to work on.

Start Your Way

Do you take a gander at the lives of individuals around you and can't help thinking about how they accomplished the sort of life that they have when your own appears to feel a tad bit of a mistake? Assume control over rolling out an improvement and be the one in control.

Numerous individuals accomplish a similar work each and every day and they feel totally content with that. Be that as it may, in the event that you can't resist thinking how you are releasing your capability to squander and have this psyche want for more rush and activity, it is an unquestionable requirement to place in some certain activity into your framework.

Assume control over towards objectives that are more aggressive. On the off chance that this is the line of believed that you have at the present time, at that point, it is significant that you don't permit the circumstance's latency to pull you down. Never have a go at coming up with pardons and defend why you are as yet not making the most out of your possibilities. On the off chance that you have this consuming fire in your heart and you realize that you can get things done, ensure that you don't permit this ability to just go to squander. To loan you some assistance in deciding whether you are truly upbeat, agreeable and fulfilled in your present status, there are a few inquiries that you need to answer first:

- Are you somebody who endeavors things and simply leave them when you are halfway? Did you become familiar with certain abilities and start a few courses however never put them without hesitation?
- Do you disdain being pushed or rushed? Is it true that you are continually deferring the conveyances of the venture that you handle and never feel tried with respect to the postponement?
- Do you like setting up a great deal for your outings or house rearrangements?

- Do you wait before and think back with aching to those occasions when things have been something more?

- Do you feel that time is restricted for the things you need to do yet you actually go through hours after our own sitting idle or moving like a zombie?

- Do you love watching the lives of those popular and rich individuals? Did you actually ask why you want to gain proficiency with the insights regarding the lives of others and whether you are simply attempting to make up for in the shortcoming of your life similarly?

- Are you longing for doing historic things however you never get down into doing them?

At the point when a few of these inquiries found a yes for a solution, the time has come for you begin considering things that you can do to split away from the idleness, shut down all your whimpering and assume responsibility for your life.

By being accountable for your life, you will be the one to settle on the decisions on how you see your present circumstance. You need to figure out how to quit tricking yourself and begin to understand that the wellbeing of the shore you are in might really be more harming to yourself than your opinion. Go out there and be in full control of your life!

Chapter 2
Motivation determination

Inspirations have a major effect in your life. There are various kinds of inspiration and every last one of them is exceptional in its own particular manner. Study inspiration and choose which one of them is your help.

Understanding Different Kinds of Motivation

What drives individuals to do the things that they do? For what reason are a few people fruitful while others are disappointments? The correct response for this likely lies in their inspirations. Indeed, even since the beginning, you are now mindful that inspiration is the thing that prompts you to learn and display different sorts of conduct, invigorating you to achieve new fruitful accomplishments. What's more, when you develop and develop more seasoned while experiencing the various phases of your life, you additionally will gain proficiency with the things that inspire you and the things that don't.

Inspiration Defined

When all is said in done, inspiration is being characterized as the power which urges individuals to activity. This is the thing that drives you to try sincerely and pushes you to succeed. It enormously impacts your conduct just as your capacity to achieve objectives.

Inspiration comes in various structures, with each and every one of them impacting an individual's conduct. No particular sort of inspiration works for all individuals. People have various characters similarly that the caring inspiration that affects their conduct likewise does, as well.

Sorts of Motivation

- Fear – This sort of inspiration accompanies results and this is typically utilized when another sort of inspiration, the motivator inspiration, turns into a disappointment. Negative outcomes or discipline are types of this inspiration. This is normally utilized for inspiring the understudies in instructive framework and is additionally utilized in expert settings for spurring representatives. At the point when rules are broken or the set objective was not accomplished, you will be punished here and there.
- Incentive – This type of inspiration is one that includes rewards, either as cash or not. Many individuals are driven when they realize that they will get a prize when they arrived at an objective or target. Advancements and

rewards are extraordinary instances of this sort of inspiration.

- Growth – The need to develop yourself is a sort of inside inspiration. The passionate longing of knowing yourself more just as the rest of the world is something that can be a solid inspiration structure. Humans by nature will always seek to grow and learn. Motivation for growth is seen in a person's yearning for change. A lot of people are wired by their personalities or upbringing to always look for change either in their knowledge or internal or external environment. Stagnation is considered as both undesirable and negative.

- Achievement – Also called drive for competency, accomplishment inspiration is the place where you are headed to achieve your objectives and take on new difficulties. It is the point at which you need to improve your abilities and demonstrate your competency not exclusively to other people yet additionally to yourself. By and large, this sensation of accomplishment and achievement is something that has an inborn nature.

- Social – many individuals are persuaded by various social variables. It can really be the craving to be acknowledged or have a place with a specific companion gathering or the longing to identify with others in your current circumstance or the world in general. You have this inborn need of feeling associated with others, and the requirement for alliance and acknowledgment. An energetic and real craving or contributing and creating an alternate in others' lives can likewise be another type of this social inspiration. At the point when you have the aching of making a commitment to your general surroundings, this is an indication that social variables propel you.

- Power – Power inspiration can either be as want of controlling others or want for self-governance. You need to have power over your life and settle on the decisions. You make progress toward your capacity of coordinating the way that you live now and how your life will unfurl later on. Likewise, a few people aim of controlling others around them. A few people have a more grounded want for this contrasted with the rest. In certain examples, this force needing can make individuals display shameless, unlawful or destructive conduct. In certain circumstances, the aching for power is as basic as the craving of influencing others' conduct. It is the point at which you simply need individuals to do what you need dependent on your plan and how you need action items.

By deciding your inspirations, you will have the option to pinpoint the particular kind of inspiration that will be best with regards to rousing the needed conduct either in yourself or in others.

Chapter 3
Goals Arrangement

To assume responsibility for your life, you need to ensure that you are clear with regards to your objectives. Putting together them in their method of significance is the most ideal approach to guarantee that you will arrive at the large thing. This section will give you a short guide for orchestrating your objectives.

Whenever you have set down to making your life's objectives, you will unquestionably have a few troubles in really beginning. There is a high possibility that you will wind up failing to remember the objectives that you made. You will likewise think that it's difficult to recall the more modest objectives that you need to finish for you to arrive at your large objectives. Or on the other hand you most likely believe that you are not generally gaining any ground since you didn't record anything.

Orchestrating and sorting out your objectives will without a doubt be of incredible assistance for you to contact them quicker and simultaneously know about the advancement that you are making.

Steps for Goal Organization

Things being what they are, how would you go about objective association? What Do You Plan to Achieve?

Above all else, you need to acknowledge and understand the way that instructive, monetary and vocation objectives will require additional time and exertion contrasted with different objectives. You likewise need to consider your wellbeing on the off chance that you have some actual objectives like conditioning, picking up muscle and weight reduction.

At the point when you organize your objectives, you need to begin with those that are simpler first. Objectives like doing things that you appreciate or changing your disposition are a lot simpler to be finished and can be arrived at quicker.

Likewise, never fear requesting help. You can tell others about the objectives that you have, especially when your objective is to have any kind of effect on the planet, which makes others need to loan some assistance.

Rundown down the entirety of your objectives dependent on their degree of significance and concoct a different sheet for each objective with the more modest objectives that you should achieve to arrive. Ensure that you keep the rundown of your objectives and all the things that you require to accomplish them in a solitary spot. Your cell phone can be a decent spot to keep them however other compact things will as of now work.

Chapter 4
Moving towards Goal

It isn't sufficient that you just put together and orchestrate your objectives. It is an absolute necessity that you work your way towards them each and every day or something bad might happen, all your work will go down the channel. Here, you will find the most ideal methods of accomplishing your objectives and how you should approach moving towards them.

For every day that passes, you either draw nearer to arriving at your objectives or you move a lot further away from them. Doing nothing will just move you away from your objectives. At the point when you remain still, you will lose your force and the inactivity level of your present position will increment. To get going toward your objectives, here are a few stages that you can follow:

Approaches to Reach Your Goals Every Day

- Have an away from of the things you like to accomplish. You will always be unable to move towards your objective in the event that you don't have the foggiest idea what your objective really is. Make sure that the image is understood. It is never enough that you simply need to have "a superior work" and all things considered, ensure that you obviously picture the occupation you need and why this will be superior to your present place of employment. It is likewise insufficient that you simply have an objective to act naturally utilized; rather, you need to think of a clearer image of what you will do and how this will transform yourself to improve things.

- See to it that you invest energy in imagining being effective. As a piece of getting an away from of your objective, it will be ideal to assign some an ideal opportunity for envisioning yourself in arriving at your objective. However much as could reasonably be expected, attempt to make it nitty gritty in your psyche and set aside the effort to compose your objectives in significant subtleties. Each time you want to get debilitate, have a go at going to a peaceful spot for some time and utilize the ideal opportunity for picturing your undertakings' prosperity.

- Incorporate enormous joy in achieving your objective. The subsequent stage in getting towards your objectives is partner incredible joy that you will encounter once your objectives are figured it out. It tends to be the cycle of perception's common surge in the subsequent advance. You ought to consider how you will feel once you succeed.

How is it going to be life? What sort of satisfaction would you say you will have? How are you going to celebrate? However much as could reasonably be expected, make this delight level as sensible and profound as you can. At the point when more joy is related with accomplishing your objective, it will be a lot simpler for you to escape the safe place and do all the things needed for accomplishing that objective.

- Associate extraordinary torment with the idea of disappointment. One more inspiration that will push you to your objective is the torment that you will connect with neglecting to achieve your objective. During school years, it is an inspiration that can push understudies to composing the exposition daily before its due, with the torment of bombing getting genuine to them. What agonies anticipate you when you didn't accomplish your objectives? What are the things that you won't get? By what means will this look to the individuals around you?

- How would you say you will feel about yourself? Ensure that these torments will be clear in your brain at that point use them for propelling yourself towards activity. Continuously remember that you can never maintain a strategic distance from torments yet use them to propel yourself towards your objectives.

- Do significant things consistently towards accomplishing your objectives. Start by deciding the urgent exercises that should be done to achieve your objective. You can separate every objective into a few stages and you can additionally separate these means into exercises that you need to arrive at these objectives. It is an unquestionable requirement to accomplish something day by day from your rundown. It implies that even when you are tied up in doing different things, or when you are worn out or when some surprising things burn-through your time, you need to look for a way that can help you doing one thing that can help you push ahead. Regardless of how straightforward the demonstration may be, it will help you in keeping your energy moving towards the correct way.

- Ensure that your objectives will remain at the front of your psyche. It isn't sufficient that you just have an away from of your objective in your psyche and yet, it is an unquestionable requirement that it remains at the front of your brain. There are a lot of ways that you do to remind yourself about your objective, and one smart thought is thinking of a storyboard that has photographs of the things you need to have. You can likewise utilize the schedule framework for setting updates and let them help you in keeping zeroed in on the objectives you dream to accomplish.

These are the six basic advances that you can follow to move towards your objectives. Ensure that you put them to activity.

Chapter 5
Time Management

Dealing with your time appropriately is one thing that you need to dominate on the off chance that you need to totally be accountable for your life. Time itself is life so ensure that you read this article to know the significance of time the board.

On the off chance that you are one of those individuals who will in general take as much time as necessary for truly, you will definitely ask why time the board is significant. However, do you realize that this turns out to be the essential expertise that you need to learn and dominate in the event that you fantasy about being effective later on?

Without time the board, happenstance will assume control over your life. You will never be guiding your life and at last, you will wind up doing the things that others need you do to do. You will be the one in charge and you will be the one to choose precisely where you would need to go.

There are a lot of advantages that you will undoubtedly appreciate when you practice time the board. The second you totally ace it, you will have the option to work more, play more, and learn quicker than at any other time.

Significance of Time Management in Your Life

You Get Additional Productive Hours

With appropriate time the executives, you will have the advantage of having extra gainful hours. You will be more focused when you are grinding away as opposed to investing your valuable energy in tattling with your associates or randomly riding the web.

Simply envision having one extra gainful hour consistently. This is identical to five additional hours in your working week and around 250 hours in your whole year. This implies six additional long stretches of work inside a year.

You Increase Your Productivity and Efficiency

With time the board, you will have the option to work more enthusiastically in a comparative period of time as others. At the point when more work is done, you will likewise learn more things and for that, you will gather more experience contrasted with others in the comparable measure of time contributed.

You will have the option to learn quicker how to finish your work quicker. You will be more engaged, permitting you to give significantly more consideration in each work that you do. Your advancement will be quicker contrasted with not utilizing your aptitudes in time the executives.

You Will Have More Fun and Leisure Time

On the off chance that you love life, it is an absolute necessity for you to try time the board. It is on the grounds that this will give you the possibility of making the most of your life without limit, do the things that you need to do and will encounter those that you need to encounter.

Since your working hours will turn out to be more gainful, you will be working less while as yet accomplishing more. It will at that point result to all the more available time that you can go through with your family and do your #1 relaxation exercises. At the same time, you will likewise find out about the embodiment of good unwinding that will result to better happiness and improved energy for finishing your work.

You Will Control Your Life Better

The last yet certainly not minimal advantage of utilizing time the board is that you will deal with the way that your life goes or basically, you can assume responsibility for your life totally. You will have improved impression of the work that you can accomplish and the work that should be finished.

You will turn out to be better coordinated, keeping cutoff times from transforming into an issue. You will never encounter cutoff time crises and all things considered; you will invest more energy for unwinding while others are as yet worried with their work.

Never be anxious about the possibility that that you will wind up firm or unbending with your time since it will really be the specific inverse. You will have more opportunity since you will be less reliant outwardly occasions for controlling your time. With time the board, you will be the one to control your time and not another person.

Chapter 6
Why not to procrastinate?

Delaying has consistently been a word that is being viewed as negative and this is for a valid justification. Stalling with your undertakings is never something worth being thankful for and this part will edify you with the disservices of this attribute.

Procrastination and Its Different Negative Effects in Your Life

Procrastinating, as a rule, is something that will make you put off your assignment until the latest possible time. On the off chance that achievement or dread of disappointment gives you the restless inclination when a troublesome errand comes your direction, simply envision the uneasiness you will feel when the cutoff time of your basic undertaking is quick drawing nearer however you have not finished it yet on the grounds that you procrastinated.

Envision having a few assignments that you need to finish at around a comparative time. Without a doubt, apprehension will be your first inclination when you consider being in such circumstances that you have placed yourself in or will place yourself in view of your off-base choices.

For various reasons, individuals will in general put off things consistently until the last possible moment and each time you do, you generally have the comparable anxious inclination that will assume control over your body. It is significant for you to stop dawdling for your psychological, enthusiastic and actual prosperity. In the event that you won't be extra cautious, its belongings can harm your life and make you vulnerable to various results.

Contrary Effects of Procrastination in Your Personal Life

It is very unfortunate that you keep getting your body through this sort of pressure since it isn't only undesirable for yourself alone for this likewise puts an undesirable strain on the various connections of your life.

In light of studies, it has been proposed that uneasiness can bargain your invulnerable framework, which can make your body inclined to contaminations and sicknesses. At the point when you feel restless of things, you lose your capacity to center which can expand the odds of being engaged with various mishaps.

When you decide putting things off instead of dealing with them, what you are actually doing is creating more work for yourself down the road. And when you have more work, you will feel more stressed due to the backlogged work that you still need to do.

Surely, you know that simply avoiding completing your task today does not necessarily mean that you will no longer need to do it the next day.

Some people think that when they go to sleep at night, you will wake up the next day with the task completed like magic. But you need to take note that this is not how things work. Instead, you will wake up with a much heavier burden compared to the previous day. This anxiety or stress that you feel for a long period of time will result to situations that are more situations, including depression and other types of mental illnesses.

While moderate stress can be good for you as this makes you more competitive and drive you to become more innovative, this can also drive you to a mental institution before you know it. If you will not learn how to better manage your stress, this can cause depression and similar mental issues which will make it even harder to cope with your life.

At the point when you persuade yourself to tarry, you are not generally doing anything other than misleading yourself into believe that different things hold more significance than what you should do right now. One normal motivation behind why you are quickly drawn off-track is because of your absence of discretion.

For you to make the most out of your life, you need to figure out how to control yourself better, especially when individual accounting records are concerned. At the point when you stall while covering your tabs, it will result to a mounting obligation that can lastingly affect your life. This obligation won't simply influence only you yet additionally your youngsters and your family all in all.

For example, if some awful obligations have aggregated, quite possibly this obligation will be passed down to your youngsters, making them liable for it. Doubtlessly, this is anything but a sort of weight that you will need to put on your youngsters basically in light of the fact that you have been reckless. On the off chance that you don't pay your home loan as expected, the home loan organization or the bank will go on with home abandonment.

It is only simple for you to reveal to yourself that you will cover the tab later or send the check over the mail tomorrow. Notwithstanding, what isn't simple is managing the negative impacts of sending the check in mail later and losing your home as the outcome.

Negative Effects of Procrastination in Other Aspects of Your Life

The drawbacks of delaying are not focused on your funds alone however there are additionally some genuine outcomes that it can provide for your wellbeing. How frequently did you hear accounts of others experiencing hurts and dodging visits to the specialist? The second they go to their primary care physician; it will simply be the consequence of supreme need and they will at that point discover that it is now something genuine.

There are additionally stories when luckily, the individual visits the specialist simply in the perfect chance to realize that it is as of now dangerous yet there are likewise occasions when they are not so fortunate. Or on the other hand what about when you experience the ill effects of a toothache and disregarded it as opposed to fixing it with the basic sealant yet will currently require a root channel? Everybody delays at some level yet guarantee that it won't prompt something perilous.

You can likewise see the impacts of dawdling at work. At your working environment, you should beat cutoff times that can help you remain on your undertaking and sort out your outstanding task at hand.

Genuine entanglements anticipate you when you put off unwanted errands. For example, you can be viewed as somebody awkward, questionable or basically languid. It is an unquestionable requirement that when you have obligation in your work, you need to execute this as well as could be expected for your uprightness and relationship with your collaborators and partners.

In your life, there are a great deal of things that you need to do to ensure that you will work throughout each and every day. These errands can go from something as basic as cleaning up or covering your tabs. However, regardless of how an insignificant an assignment may appear; it is significant that you avoid tarrying however much as could be expected. You can be hundred percent sure that delaying your assignments will quite often prompt emerging distinctive sudden issues. Along these lines, while you have the inclination to do different things than the employment sitting tight for you, you need to lock in and manage the one you are confronted with prior to whatever else.

Chapter 7
Self-Discipline

What is simply the genuine pith discipline in your life? By what method will it have the option to help you in arriving at your objectives and having a full control of your life? This last part will open your brain to the genuine substance of self-control and why you need it in your life.

The Importance and Benefits of Self Discipline

One of the most valuable and significant abilities that everybody should have is in all honesty self-control. This ability is indispensable in for all intents and purposes all parts of an individual's life and keeping in mind that a great many people know its significance, a couple truly make moves in reinforcing it.

In opposition to mainstream thinking, this quality isn't tied in with being brutal to yourself or driving a confined and restricted way of life. Self-control is about poise, an indication of inward strength and having full control of your responses, your activities and yourself overall.

Self-control blesses you the intensity of adhering to the choices you make and finishing them no compelling reason to adjust your perspective and hence, making it one of the most pivotal necessities to accomplish your objectives.

With this sort of ability, you can protect with every one of your arrangements and choices until you contact them all. This will likewise show itself as your internal strength that will assist you with combatting addictions, sluggishness, hesitation and letting your finish in all that you do.

Among its essential qualities is the capacity of dismissing moment delight and satisfaction for a greater addition that will require investing more energy and exertion to accomplish it.

There are a ton of issues and difficulties in life that will obstruct your way towards accomplishment and achievement and for you to transcend these, you need to act with both constancy and persistence and this will obviously call for self-restraint.

Having self-restraint is something that can prompt confidence and fearlessness and subsequently, this will prepare for fulfillment and satisfaction to come into your life.

Then again, when you don't have self-control, this can prompt misfortune, disappointment, relationship and medical issues, stoutness just as different issues.

It is additionally an ability that can prove to be useful for defeating addictions, dietary issues, drinking, smoking and other negative propensities. It is significant that you cause yourself to practice your body, to sit and contemplate, create spic and span abilities and for otherworldly development, reflection, and personal growth.

As referenced before, the vast majority are truly mindful of the advantages and significance of self-restraint yet a couple of them make real strides for creating and reinforcing it. In any case, you can make this capacity more grounded like the remainder of different aptitudes. It very well may be finished with the correct activities and preparing that you can undoubtedly discover in various sources.

Basically, self-control will help you:

- Avoid imprudent and impulsively activities.

- Overcome dawdling and sluggishness.

- Fulfill guarantees that you make to yourself just as to other people.

- Go to your rec center, go for a stroll and swim regardless of your brain advising you to simply remain at home and sit before the TV.

- Continue dealing with a specific undertaking even route after the main surge of energy has just disappeared.

- Overcome your propensity for unreasonable viewing of TV.

- Continue with your eating regimen and oppose the allurement of eating nourishments that can make you fat.

- Wake up early each day.

- Meditate routinely.

Chapter 8
The Dominating Rationale

Call yourself to be solid to the point that nothing may interfere with your genuine feelings of serenity. To talk wellbeing, joy and success to every individual you meet. To cause every one of your colleagues to feel that there's something in them.

To see the radiant side of everything and make your idealism work out. To accept simply the best, to turn out just generally advantageous, and to envision simply the best. To be even as energetic about the accomplishment of others as you are about your own. To clear out the mistakes of the past and push on to the more prominent accomplishments of things to come.

To wear a playful face consistently and give each living animal you meet a grin. To introduce such a huge amount of time to the improvement of yourself that you've no an ideal opportunity to thump others. To be too large for stress, excessively honorable for rage, excessively solid for fear; and too glad to even consider allowing the difficult situation.

To appreciate yourself and to shout this reality to the world, not in noisy words but rather in great deeds. To live in the confidence that the entire world is your ally inasmuch as you're consistent with the best that is in you.

Our opinion

The reason for the going with pages will be to dissect the entire idea of man, discover all the powers in his ownership, regardless of whether they be clear or covered up, alive or torpid, and to introduce strategies through which each one of those powers might be applied in making the life of each individual more extravagant, more prominent and better. To make each period of this work as helpful as conceivable to the most elevated number conceivable, not one assertion will be made that all can't comprehend, and not one thought will be introduced that anyone can't matter to everyday life.

We as a whole wish to understand what we truly have both in the physical, the psychological and the profound, and we wish to see how the components and powers inside us might be applied in the best way. Its outcomes in pragmatic life that we wish, and we're not consistent with the race or ourselves till we figure out how to use the forces inside us so successfully, that the best outcomes conceivable inside the conceivable outcomes of human instinct are guaranteed.

The issue before us is to comprehend what is in us and how to use what is in us. In the event that we just realized how to use these forces, we could accomplish basically whatever we may have in sight, and not just understand our desires to the fullest degree, however similarly reach even our most noteworthy objective. In spite of the fact that this may appear to be a solid explanation, all things considered, we're constrained to concede that it's actual even in its fullest sense, and not one individual may neglect to understand his needs and arrive at his objective, after he has figured out how to use the forces that are in him.

The more we study the lives of people who have accomplished, and the more we study our own experience day by day, the surer we become that there's no explanation whatever why any individual shouldn't understand every one of his desires and considerably more.

We need to understand what we are, before we may know and use what we in characteristically have. Man is assembled of self-image, awareness and structure. Man is body, brain and soul. Man is incorporated of uniqueness and character.

Before we pass to the more down to earth side of the subject, we will think that its productive to view quickly these varying thoughts concerning the idea of man. At the point when the normal individual utilizes the expression "inner self," he imagines that he's managing something that is covered so profoundly in the theoretical that it might have little effect if we get it.

This, anyway isn't accurate, in light of the fact that the inner self should act before any cycle may occur anyplace in the human framework, and the personality needs to start the new before any development might be taken. Also, it's extremely vital to understand that the intensity of will to control the powers we have, relies straightforwardly upon how completely cognizant we are of the self-image as the decision guideline inside us. It's absolutely fundamental to relate all idea, all, feeling and all activities of brain or character with the personality.

The initial move in this association, is to understand "the conscience" in all that you do, and to think consistently about "the self-image", as being you - the preeminent you. On the off chance that you think, understand that it's "the inner self" that started the idea. At whatever point you act, perceive that it's "the personality" that offers activity to that activity, and at whatever point you consider yourself or endeavor to be aware of yourself, perceive that "the inner self" possesses the seat of your whole field of cognizance. An alternate critical basic is to certify quietly as far as you could tell that no doubt about it".

Also, as you confirm this think about "the personality" similar to the decision standard in your entire world, as being particular or more and better than all else in your being, and as being you, yourself, in the most elevated, biggest, and most exhaustive sense.

You subsequently lift yourself up, figuratively speaking, to the peak of marvelous singularity; you enthrone yourself; you become consistent with yourself; you place yourself where you have a place. Through this training, you not just find yourself to be the expert of your entire life, however you advance all your cognizant activities to that grand state in your awareness. On the off chance that you need to control and direct the powers you have, you need to act from the seat of your being, or put in an unexpected way, from that cognizant point in your psychological world wherein all intensity of order, heading and activity continues. You need to act, not as a body, not as a character, not as a, mind, but rather as "the personality".

At the point when we examine the psyche of the normal individual, we find that they regularly recognize themselves with brain or body. They think either that they're body or that they're mind, and subsequently they may control neither the brain nor the body.

"The conscience" in their inclination is lowered in a lot of thoughts, some of which are valid and some of which are not, and their idea is ordinarily constrained by those thoughts without getting any bearing from that rule inside them that by itself was proposed to provide guidance.

An alternate method that is profoundly significant in this association is to take a couple of moments every day and attempt to feel that you - "the self-image" - are above brain and body, yet from a specific perspective, particular from psyche and body. This training will give you what may be named an ideal awareness. Likewise, all your psychological activities will, from that time on, come straightforwardly from "the inner self"; and on the off chance that you'll keep on remaining over all such activities consistently, you'll have the option to control them and direct them completely.

At the point when "the sense of self" watches out upon life we have straight-forward awareness. At the point when "the conscience" looks on its own situation in life we have reluctance, and when "the self-image" turns upward into the unfathomability of genuine we have grandiose awareness.

In basic cognizance, you're just witting of those things that exist ostensibly to yourself, yet when you begin to get aware of yourself as a particular element, you begin to create reluctance. At the point when you begin to direct your concentration toward the extraordinary inside and begin to turn upward into the genuine wellspring, everything being equal, you become aware of that world that apparently exists inside all universes, and when you enter upon this experience, you're on the borderland of vast awareness, the most intriguing subject that is ever been known.

Before, we have continually used the articulation, "I have a spirit," which normally infers the conviction that "I'm a body"; thus, profoundly has this thought become fixed in the ordinary psyche that almost everybody thinks about the body at whatever point the expression "me" or "myself "is utilized. However, in this mentality of psyche the individual isn't over the actual conditions of thought and feeling; indeed, he's pretty much lowered in what may be known as a heap of actual realities and considerations, of which he has almost no control.

You can't control anything in your life, be that as it may, till you're above it. You can't control what is in your body till you understand that you're over your body. You can't control what is in your cerebrum till you understand that you're over your brain, and subsequently nobody may utilize the powers inside them to any degree inasmuch as they consider themselves being limited solely in the body. The spirit is simply the man, and that the sense of self is the focal standard of the spirit; or to use another articulation, the spirit, including "the conscience", establishes the singularity, and that noticeable something through which uniqueness discovers articulation, contains the character.

On the off chance that you wish to fathom your powers, and gain that mind-blowing disposition important to the order of your powers, train yourself to believe that you are a spirit, yet don't consider the spirit something ambiguous or puzzling. Consider the spirit just like the individual you and all that that articulation may conceivably infer. Train yourself to imagine that you are expert of brain and body, as your above psyche and body, and have the ability to use all that is as a primary concern and body.

Chapter 9
Regulating the Powers

Man is ever looking for strength. It's the resilient man that successes. It's the man with might that scales the statures. To be solid is to be brilliant; and it's the advantage of significance to fulfill each want, each aspiration, each need. Yet, strength isn't for the couple of alone; it's for all, and the best approach to strength is basic. Go right now to the peaks of the strength you presently have, and whatever may happen don't descend.

Try not to debilitate under difficulty. Take steps to remain as solid, as decided and as exceptionally enthused during the most obscure evening of difficulty as you are during the most splendid day of thriving. Try not to feel baffled when matters appear to be frustrating. Keep the eye single upon a similar splendid future paying little heed to conditions, conditions or occasions. Try not to lose heart when matters turn out badly. Proceed with undisturbed in your unique immovability to make everything go right. To be overwhelmed by difficulty and compromising disappointment is to lose strength; to consistently remain in a similar elevated, decided state of mind is to never-endingly become stronger. The one who never breaks when matters are against him will get more grounded and more grounded till everything will enjoyment to be for him. He will eventually have all the strength he may want or require. Be perpetually solid and you'll everlastingly be more grounded.

Taking Command

At whatever point you think or at whatever point you feel, at whatever point you talk, at whatever point you act, or whatever may be going on in your life, your incomparable thought should be that you're above it all, better than it all, and have order, all things considered, you simply should make this higher ground in all move, thought and awareness before you may control yourself and direct, for viable purposes, the powers you have.

Thusly, "the personality", the spirit and the independence being one, is similarly as significant as anything that may be said from this point forward regarding the use of the powers in man to reasonable activity. at the point when we figure out how to perceive that we, normally, involve a place that is above brain and body, this piece of the subject will be discovered more intriguing than all else, and its application more productive.

We may characterize uniqueness all the more completely by expressing that it's the undetectable man and that everything in man that is imperceptible has a place with his singularity.

The singularity starts, that controls or coordinates. Thusly, to control and use a power in your own framework, you need to comprehend and create singularity.

Your independence should be clarified cut, decided and positive. You need to continually perceive what you are and what you wish, and you should continually be resolved to make sure about what you wish. It's uniqueness that makes you not the same as any remaining coordinated substances, and it's a profoundly evolved personality that enables you to stand out, and it's the level of character that you have that figures out what position you're to possess on the planet.

On the off chance that you see a man or lady who's extraordinary, who seems to stand out, and who's an imperative thing about them that nobody else appears to have, you've someone whose personality is profoundly evolved, and you similarly have someone who will positively shape the world. Take two people of like force, capacity and productivity, yet with this distinction. In the one personality is exceptionally evolved, while in the other it isn't.

You know straightforwardly which one of these two will arrive at the best places in the realm of achievement; and the explanation is that the person who has singularity lives above brain and body, in this way having the option to order and direct the powers a lot of psyche and body.

The individual, notwithstanding, whose uniqueness is powerless, lives pretty much down as a top priority and body, and instead of controlling brain and body, is continually being influenced by everything from the external that may enter their cognizance.

At whatever point you discover somebody who's accomplishing something beneficial, who's making an impression, who's pushing ahead toward more noteworthy and better things, you discover the distinction solid, positive and exceptionally created. It's along these lines significant that you concentrate on the advancement of a solid, positive personality on the off chance that you wish to prevail on the planet.

A negative or powerless independence generally gets just what others choose to give, yet a firm, solid, positive, very much created uniqueness, in actuality controls the boat of their life and predetermination, and ultimately will pick up ownership of what they need.

To create independence, the principal vital is to give "the sense of self" it's actual and grand situation in your psyche. At whatever point you view yourself as, see yourself as being and living and acting in the amazing demeanor. Make each want good, each feeling good, each idea good, and each activity of brain good. To make your desires particular and positive, you'll likewise will in general invigorate and positivism to your character.

A valuable procedure is to picture in your cerebrum your own best thought of what a solid, all around created personality would be, and afterward see yourself as getting increasingly more like that. We step by step develop into the resemblance of that which we consider the most. Hence, in the event that you've a truly away from of a profoundly evolved distinction, and think a great deal of that uniqueness with a solid, positive need to grow such an independence, you'll slowly move towards that.

In short, whatever we do in attempting to control and direct the forces we have, we need to enter the more profound existence of those forces, with the goal that we can oversee the propensities. It's the manner in which those inclinations stream that decides results, and as we may coordinate those ebbs and flows in any capacity that we need, we normally infer that we may make sure about whatever results we need.

Chapter 10
Practical Action

Man lives to move ahead, to move forward is to live more. To live more is to be more and accomplish more; and its being and doing that builds up the way to bliss. The more you are the more you do, the more extravagant your life, the better your euphoria. However, being and doing must in every case live respectively as one.

To endeavor to be a lot and make an effort not to do much is to find life a desolate waste. To endeavor to do a lot and do whatever it takes not to be much is to see life a weight as excessively substantial and repetitive to bear.

The being of much gives the vital inspiration and the fundamental capacity to the doing of a lot. The doing of much gives the basic articulation to the being of a lot. Furthermore, it's the delivering of being through the demonstration of doing that produces bliss. Being a lot of gives limit with respect to doing a lot.

Doing a lot of offers indication to the most extravagant and the best that is inside us. Furthermore, the more we better the extravagance of that which is inside us, the more we better our satisfaction, if we increment, in a similar extent, the outflow of that more noteworthy lavishness.

Utilizing the Mind

In the current age, it's the intensity of brain that runs the world, and thus it's obvious that he who's procured the best utilization of the intensity of psyche, will understand the best achievement, and arrive at the most noteworthy spots that fulfillment and achievement hold coming up. The one who wins is the one who may apply in pragmatic life each piece of his psychological capacity, and who may make each activity of his brain tell.

We sporadically question why there are so numerous skilled men and praiseworthy ladies who don't arrive at those spots in life that they seem to merit, however the appropriate response is basic. They don't matter the intensity of brain as they should. Their capacities and characteristics are either confused or applied uniquely to some extent. These people, nonetheless, shouldn't allow themselves to get disappointed with destiny, yet should recall that every person who figures out how to utilize the intensity of their cerebrum will arrive at their objective; they'll understand their craving and will emphatically win.

Extensively, we may state that the intensity of psyche is the Sum Total of the multitude of powers of the psychological world, including those powers that are utilized during the time spent reasoning. The intensity of brain incorporates the intensity of the will, the intensity of need, the intensity of feeling, and the intensity of thought. It remembers cognizant activity for every one of its stages and subliminal activity in the entirety of its stages.

To use the intensity of the mind, the primary basic is to coordinate each psychological activity towards the objective in view, and this bearing should not be intermittent, yet consistent. Most personalities, in any case, don't matter this law. They think about something specific one second, and about something different the following second. At a specific hour, their psychological activities work along a specific line, and at the following hour those activities work along a different line. We know, nonetheless, that every person who's really working oneself consistently toward the objective they've in view, constantly coordinates all the intensity of their idea on that objective.

In utilizing the intensity of brain, the primary inquiry to answer is the thing that we genuinely need to achieve; and when this inquiry is replied, the one thing that is needed should be fixed so plainly in idea that it could be seen by the inner being every moment.

At the point when we understand what we need, and continue to work for it with all the force that is in us, we may have confidence that we'll get it. At the point when we direct the intensity of reasoning, the intensity of will, the intensity of mental activity, the intensity of need, the intensity of yearning, all the force we have on the one thing we wish, accomplishment in a more prominent measure should be picked up.

In the event that you've a specific aspiration or a specific longing, think about that desire consistently. Keep that fantasy before your psyche continually, and don't spare a moment to make your fantasy as high as could reasonably be expected. The higher you point, the more noteworthy your achievements.

The standard is to coordinate the intensity of cerebrum on the most noteworthy mental origination of that which we intend to accomplish. Inspirational disposition is demonstrated by the sensation of a firm, decided totality all through the sensory system. At the point when each nerve feels full, solid and decided, you're in the uplifting mentality, and whatever you may do at the time will create results along the line of your aspiration. At the point when you're in a positive mood you're rarely apprehensive or upset, you're rarely disturbed or stressing; truth be told, the more certain you are the more profound your self-restraint and the better your command over your entire framework. The positive psyche is consistently in agreement with itself, while the negative brain is consistently out of congruity, and consequently loses most of its capacity.

To create positivism, it's fundamental to develop those characteristics that comprise positivism. Make it a highlight focus on what you wish to accomplish, and give that consideration immovability, tranquility and assurance. Endeavor to give profundity to each want till you feel as though all the forces of your framework were acting, not on a superficial level, but rather from the more prominent world inside.

Make each psychological activity productive, and a helpful mental activity is one that depends on a profound situated craving to create, to increment, to achieve, to accomplish - in short, to expand and more noteworthy, and to accomplish something of far more prominent incentive than has been done previously.

In the correct use of the psyche hence, these 3 fundamentals should be applied continually and altogether. To begin with, direct all the forces of brain, all the forces of thought, and all your speculation on the objective you've in view. Second, train each psychological activity to be profoundly and tranquilly certain. Third, train each psychological activity to be valuable, to be loaded up with a structure soul, to be roused with a constant craving to build up the more noteworthy, to accomplish the more prominent, to achieve the more noteworthy. At the point when you've gained these 3, you'll start to use your powers so that outcomes should follow.

At the point when we examine the psyches of individuals who have fizzled, we constantly find that they're either negative, non-valuable or untied. Their powers are dissipated, and what is in them is once in a while applied helpfully. There's a void about their character that shows negative-ness. There's a vulnerability in their outward appearance that demonstrates the nonappearance of unmistakable aspiration. There's nothing of a positive, decided nature going on in their psychological world.

What these people should do, is to continue straightforwardly to follow the 3 fundamentals referenced previously. They'll before long stop to float, and will at that point begin to make their own life, their own conditions, and their own future.

At the point when you begin to make a positive decided utilization of those forces in yourself that are as of now in Positive activity, you bring forward without hesitation powers inside you that have been resting, and as this cycle proceeds, you'll find that you'll collect volume, limit and force in your psychological world, till you at last become a psychological monster. As you begin to develop and turn out to be more fit, you'll see that you will meet better constantly openings, open doors for advancing external achievement, yet open doors for additional structure yourself up along the lines of capacity, limit and ability.

The positive and useful usage of the intensity of brain, with an unmistakable objective in sight will perpetually bring about headway, accomplishment and accomplishment, however in the event that we wish to use that power in its full limit, the activity of the psyche should be profound. Notwithstanding the correct use of the psyche, we should likewise become familiar with the full utilization of brain, and as the full use implies the utilization of the absolutely mind, the more profound mental fields and powers, just as the typical mental fields and powers, it's important to comprehend the psyche just as the cognizant.

Chapter 11
Subconscious training

At the point when you've decided what you wish to do, say to yourself 1000 times each day that you will do it. The most ideal way will before long open. You'll have the open door you need.

In the event that you would be more prominent later on than you are today, be all that you might be today. He who's his best builds up the ability to be better. He who experience his beliefs is creating a daily existence that truly is ideal.

There's nothing in your life that you can't change, adjust or better when you figure out how to direct your idea. Our fate isn't outlined for us by some external force; we map it out for ourselves. Our opinion and do in the present choose what will befall us later on.

Hidden Thoughts

At the point when we go ahead to prepare the subliminal for exceptional outcomes, we should consistently keep with the accompanying law: The psyche reacts to the impressions, the recommendations, the needs, the expectations and the bearings of the cognizant brain. At such at such critical times, should be quiet and should be aware of that better, better something inside.

At the point when you need to guide the psyche to create actual wellbeing, first picture an away from of wonderful wellbeing. Attempt to feel fit as a fiddle in your brain and afterward let that feeling sink into your whole actual framework. At whatever point you feel infection going ahead, you may stop it from really developing by this straightforward strategy. In the event that the inner mind is coordinated to grow more wellbeing, added powers of wellbeing will before long begin to come from inside, and cancel any problem or sickness that may be very nearly getting a traction in the body.

Continuously review that whatever is engraved on the inner mind will after some time be communicated from the psyche; and where the actual conditions that you need to eliminate are little, enough psyche force might be excited to reestablish brief request and completeness.

At the point when the condition you need to eliminate has proceeded for quite a while, notwithstanding, rehashed endeavors may be needed to make the inner mind act in the issue. However, on the off chance that you keep on guiding the inner mind to remove that condition, it emphatically will be eliminated.

The psyche doesn't just have the ability to eliminate unacceptable conditions from the physical or mental state. It might moreover create those better conditions that we need, and grow further those appropriate conditions that we as of now have. To apply the law for this reason, profoundly want those conditions that you do need, and have an unmistakable thought in your brain with regards to what you need those conditions to be. In introducing the subliminal headings for anything wanted, we ought to consistently have improvement as a primary concern.

Whatever we consider profoundly or seriously, the inner mind will ingest and grow further. Consequently, on the off chance that we think about our failings, deficiencies or unfortunate propensities, the psyche will take them up and give them more life and action than they ever had previously. In the event that there's anything that we wish to transform, we should just continue to develop what we need and clear out totally what we wish to clear out. At the point when the great advances, the terrible vanishes.

On the off chance that you have some incredible yearning that you wish to acknowledge, direct the subliminal commonly consistently and consistently before you rest; and in case you're resolved, those things will be approaching. It's basic to recollect that we need to fixate on the one thing needed. On the off chance that your brain dissipates, you'll befuddle the inner mind and it won't be made sure about.

On the off chance that there's any situation you want to dispose of direct the inner mind to give you that data to discover an exit plan. The psyche can. We as a whole recollect the maxim, "Where there is a will there is a way", and it's actual. In the event that there's any ability that you wish to develop further, direct the subliminal every day, and as regularly as could reasonably be expected, to amplify that ability and to expand its capacity. The entire psyche, cognizant and subliminal, has the ability to determine any issue that may come up, or give the fundamental available resources through which we may complete anything. Careful discipline brings about promising results. The more you train the inner mind to work with you, the less complex it becomes to get the psyche to react to your headings.

Start by accepting that it can do what you've told it to do, and kill question totally. Take a few minutes every day and propose to the subliminal what you wish to have done. Be completely genuine in that issue; be resolved; have vast confidence, and you may anticipate results. Continuously be quiet when thinking or proposing to the psyche, and it's especially significant that you be profoundly quiet before you rest. Try not to allow any thought, proposal or desire to enter the subliminal except if it's something that you truly need, and here we should recollect that every thought, want or outlook that is profoundly felt will enter the psyche. When there are no outcomes, don't lose confidence. Attempt once more.

Continuously be set up to give these techniques adequate time. Regardless of whether you get results when you need or not keep giving your headings every day, completely anticipating results. Be resolved in every exertion you make toward this path, however don't be over-restless.

Give specific bearings to the subliminal every day for the consistent improvement of brain, character and character. Each exertion you may cause will to acquire its normal outcomes proper method, given you're generally quiet, even, tenacious, profoundly ready and amicable in the entirety of your contemplations and activities.

Chapter 12
Law of Attraction

Life is improvement and the object of right believing is to propel that development. Give less time endeavoring to change the assessments of others, and additional time endeavoring to improve your own life.

Daily routine turns into the manner in which it is experienced; and man may live the manner in which he wishes to live when he figures out how to think what he wishes to think. Make your own idea and you become what you wish to become as your idea makes you.

We as a whole realize that man is as he might suspect. At that point we should think just such contemplations as will in general make us what we wish to be. The mystery of right reasoning is found in continually keeping the inner being upon the more prominent and the better no matter what.

Accumulate the Correct Thoughts

Examination in the otherworldly field has proven the way that man is as he might suspect, that he becomes his opinion, and that his opinion in the present, chooses what he's to get later on. Also, that since he may improve his idea, he may in this way totally change himself along any line.

Nonetheless, the lion's share who attempt to apply this law don't prevail generally, the explanation being that instead of working totally upon the rule that man is as he might suspect, they continue in the conviction that man is the thing that he thinks he is. From the start, there may appear to be no distinction between the rule that man is as he might suspect and the conviction that man is as he might suspect he seems to be, however close examination will reveal the way that the last is totally false.

Man isn't what he thinks he is, as character, mindset and character are not dictated by genuine beliefs. It's the idea of the heart that makes the individual man what he is and not by his opinion about himself in the field of simple genuine belief. Its abstract idea that makes you what you are; yet to feel that you're in this manner or thereabouts, won't really make you accordingly or somewhere in the vicinity. To create abstract idea, you should act straightforwardly upon the psyche, yet it is absurd to expect to dazzle the inner mind while you're framing emotions about your own self.

A simple assertion about yourself won't influence or change the inner mind, thus long as the psyche remains unaltered, you'll remain unaltered. While you're pondering your outside or individual self you're following up on the target, yet to adjust yourself you should follow up on the abstract.

You may imagine that you're well, however you won't make sure about wellbeing till you think considerations that produce wellbeing. You may tirelessly attest that you're well, yet insofar as you live in dissension, disarray, stress, concern and other wrong moods, you'll be wiped out.

It isn't what we state in our considerations, yet what we provide for our contemplations that choose results. To create wellbeing, figured itself should be invigorating and healthy. It needs to contain the nature of wellbeing, and the very existence of wellbeing.

This, in any case, is absurd except if the psyche is aware of wellbeing when such idea is being created. To just feel that you're well won't show the psyche to comprehend the laws of life and wellbeing, nor will that reasoning, place you in concordance with those laws.

You may accept that your brain is splendid and might attempt most troublesome assignments in the conviction that you're equivalent to the event, yet the inquiry is if your origination of brilliancy is extraordinary or little. On the off chance that your origination of brilliancy is pretty much nothing, you may be all in all correct to that degree in reasoning you're splendid; that is, you may be splendid to the extent your comprehension of brilliancy goes.

If that is adequate to complete the undertaking that is before you is an alternate inquiry. Your assessment of your intellectual ability may be incredible, yet in the event that actually knowledge for you is crude, your insight creating thought will likewise be crude. Try not to call yourself splendid whenever, or don't view yourself as ailing in brilliancy. Simply fix the psychological eye on outright brilliancy, and want with all the intensity of brain and soul to continue forever into higher strides of that brilliancy.

Man is the outcome, not of convictions or assessments, but rather of the nature of the relative multitude of mental activities that are grinding away all through the entire brain. Man is as he might suspect in each idea, and not what he thinks he is in at least one detached pieces of his own self.

You may feel that you're acceptable, however your guideline of goodness may not be right. You're just on a par with the amount of all your great considerations, and these might be expanded in number uncertainly via preparing the brain to continually fill in the awareness of outright goodness. To fill in the cognizance of goodness, watch out for the best origination of total goodness.

From the previous, it's clear that man is as he might suspect, and not unavoidably what he thinks he is. Your opinion about yourself is consistently target thought, and simple target thought is feeble to modify anything in your temperament.

To change yourself you should go to that profundity of brain where the reasons for your own condition exist. Yet, your brain won't enter the profundity of the inside inasmuch as your idea is on a superficial level and your idea will be on a superficial level insofar as you're contemplating your own self.

The mystery in this manner isn't to frame assessments about yourself or to view yourself as being hence or something like that, yet to shape greater originations of standards and characteristics. Enter the wealth of reality and you'll think more extravagant musings. Disregard the limits, the shortcomings and the imperfections of your own self just as your surface assessments of yourself, and enter intellectually into the grandness, the splendor, everything being equal.

Look to pick up a bigger comprehension of the magnificence of all life.

He who thinks healthy contemplations and healthy considerations just, will get empowering and healthy. Such musings will reserve the privilege to deliver wellbeing, and contemplations never neglect to do what they have the ability to do. Spot in real life the basic inner mind thought and the foreseen results will perpetually follow.

Chapter 13
Desires achievement

The way that you've neglected to get the lesser demonstrates decisively that you merit the more noteworthy. So thusly, dry those tears and go looking for the more attractive prize.

Tally nothing lost; even the day that sees "no commendable activity done" may be a day of planning and collection that will add significantly to the achievements of tomorrow. Numerous a day was made popular since nothing was done the day preceding. Understand what you want and keep on craving it. You'll get it on the off chance that you consolidate want with confidence. The intensity of want when mixed with confidence gets invulnerable. A couple of the chief reasons why so many neglects to get what they want is on the grounds that they don't have a clue what they need or on the grounds that they change their needs practically day by day.

Want and Faith

The motivation behind craving is to illuminate man what he needs at every specific second to supply the requests of progress and development in his life; and in advancing that reason, want gives articulation to its two driving capacities. The first of these is to give the powers of the human framework something unequivocal to do, and the second is to stir those powers or resources that have the natural capacity to do what can anyone does. In practicing its first capacity, want not just raises centralization of activity among the powers in man, however similarly makes those powers work for what's needed. Subsequently, it's promptly perceived why the wish, if solid, positive, decided and constant, will in general deliver the thing ached for.

In the event that you can cause all the components and forces in your being to work for the one thing that you want you are practically sure to get it. We'll take, for example, a man who isn't procuring as much as he feels that he requires. Normally, he will begin to want more cash; and we'll guess that this need gets more grounded and more grounded till it really blends each molecule of his being.

Presently what happens? He isn't just stirring a decent arrangement of dormant and unused energy; however, the entirety of his dynamic energy is getting more alive. Yet, what is the fate of this energy? It goes straightforwardly into his moneymaking resources, and watches out for better firmly the life, the influence, the limit and the productivity of those resources.

There's in each psyche a specific gathering of resources that is made commonly for monetary purposes. In certain personalities, these resources are little and languid, while in different personalities they're large and dynamic. Also, that the last kind should have the option to make more income and amass things in a more prominent measure is very common. Yet, is it conceivable to take those resources that are close to nothing and lazy and make them enormous and dynamic? Provided that this is true, the individuals who currently have limited methods may over the span of time have wealth.

To respond to this inquiry, we'll ask what it is that may stir any workforce to expand and more dynamic, and we find that it's more energy, and energy that is more alive. In any case how drowsy a workforce may be, if it's completely energized with exceptionally dynamic energy, it only should turn out to be more dynamic.

What's more, notwithstanding how little it very well may be, in the event that it keeps on getting a constant flow of added life, energy and force, every day, after quite a long time after month, after a seemingly endless amount of time after year, it doubtlessly should increment in size and limit. Furthermore, at whatever point any staff gets more noteworthy in limit and more alive in real life it will accomplish better work. It will progressively pick up in capacity and force till it has adequate capacity and capacity to deliver what you wanted.

Getting back to the man in our representation, we'll perceive how the guideline works. His moneymaking resources are close to nothing and too languid to even think about producing as much income as he needs. He begins to want more. His solid, determined longing for more income has stirred his moneymaking resources. They've gotten more grounded, more dynamic, all the more wide-wakeful and more productive. Furthermore, as a solid, wide-conscious staff may do ordinarily as great work as one that is just halfway alive, we see how his craving for more cash has enabled him to get more cash-flow.

As he proceeds with this craving, making it more grounded and more persevering, his monetary force will expand likewise, and his monetary profits keep on expanding in extent. You become like the thing you need, and when the likeness has gotten total, you'll get what you need through the law of like pulling in like.

Understand what you need, and afterward need it with all the life and force that is in you. Get your brain and your life completely excited. Tireless need will do this. It's fundamental, that your cravings proceed uninterruptedly along the lines you have chosen. You may want various things, yet proceed with each want without change, except if you locate that specific changes are fundamental to make sure about the more prominent outcomes you have as a top priority. To want one thing today and another tomorrow implies disappointment.

Leave your aspirations alone high, just verify that you're acting inside the circle of your own intrinsic limit; however, in this association it's well to recollect that your inborn limit is commonly as extraordinary as it has should be; and similarly, that it could be ceaselessly broadened.

In picking what you're to want, act sensibly, however pursue the best. In the event that the all-out intensity of want is applied upon all the components of your brain and character, what is inactive inside you'll be stimulated, created and communicated. You'll turn out to be significantly more than you are and along these lines won't just longing the best, yet have the option to be of administration to the best. Furthermore, this last truth is significant.

At the point when we need the extraordinary and the awesome, we should ask what we need to give the incredible and the great correspondingly. It isn't simply important to get the best - to understand our ideal, however it's moreover important to be so acceptable thus incredible that we may provide for the best as much as we are getting from the best.

A similar law will apply in the need or quest for intelligence, groundbreaking thoughts, better plans, better chances, more pleasing environmental factors and more ideal buddies. The craving should be persevering and strong, as solid as all the life and soul we have.

Put in an unexpected way, we should wish sufficiently hard, and we wish hard enough when our longings are adequately full and profound and solid to completely stimulate those resources that have the intrinsic capacity to satisfy those cravings.

To make each want subliminal, the psyche mind should consistently be remembered for the cycle of want; that is, at whatever point we express a longing we should think about the psyche, and consolidate the idea of that want with our psyche. Each want should be profoundly felt.

It's an incredible practice to allow each want to sink into the more profound mental life. To get capable in these strategies requires some training, however the entirety of that is important to become capable is to keep on difficult. Start by feeling your cravings totally. Make them as solid and as profound as you can, and consistently join the living activity of your craving with your idea of those resources through which you realize that want is to work.

To show: If you need better progress in your work, think about those resources that you're utilizing in your work at whatever point you give full articulation to your craving. In the event that you are a financial specialist, consider your business resources at whatever point you need more noteworthy business achievement. In case you're an artist, consider your melodic resources at whatever point you need more noteworthy capability in your music.

Simply on the off chance that your longings should be with the end goal that you don't have the foggiest idea what sorts of resources will normally be communicated, regardless. Keep on wanting what you wish; the intensity of that want, if persevering and solid, will figure out how to make your desire work out as expected. At the point when we see how want functions, and realize that it works just when it's tireless, we understand that we have discovered, an astounding mystery, yet similarly a straightforward clarification for a large number of the disappointments in life just as a considerable lot of its most noteworthy achievements. What's more, from current realities for the situation we reason that in any case what a person's condition or position may be today, in the event that they'll settle on that something better that they need, they may get it, given their desire to it is as solid as their own life and as extensive as their own spirit.

Summary

To get fruitful, think what you need to figure, notwithstanding what your environmental factors may propose; and keep on reasoning what you wish to think till that specific line of thought or activity has been finished. Desires what you wish to want and dazzle that want so profoundly on cognizance that it can't in any way, shape or form be upset by those unfamiliar cravings that environmental factors may propose; and keep on communicating that want with all the life and force that is in you till you get what you need. At the point when you realize that you're in the correct longing, don't allow anything to impact your brain to change. Take such recommendations and convert them into the craving you've just settled on, accordingly giving that want extra life and force. Never close your psyche to impressions from without. Keep the brain open to the activities of every one of those universes that may exist in your circle and endeavor to pick up significant impressions from each source, however don't indiscriminately follow those impressions.

Use them usefully in developing your own arrangement of unique idea. Think what you wish to think, thus utilize every impression you get that you pick up more noteworthy capacity to think what you need to think. Subsequently, you'll progressively get effective. We as a whole should concede that there's more in man than what is regularly communicated in the normal person. We may vary concerning the amount more, however we should agree that the more should be created, communicated and applied in everybody.

It's off-base, both to the individual and to the race, for anyone to stay in the lesser when it's conceivable to accomplish the more prominent. It's correct that we as a whole should rise to the higher, the more noteworthy and the better today.

Also, we as a whole can!!!

Good luck.

Be loving & be smiling.

Take care.